Pictorial Price Guide To
Vinyl & Plastic
Lunch Boxes & Thermoses

By Larry Aikins

© Copyright 1993
2nd Printing 1995
Larry Aikins

Published by:
L-W Book Sales
P. O. Box 69
Gas City, IN 46933

ISBN # 0-89538-015-3

Layout:David Dilley

Front Cover

Pictured are various Vinyl & Plastic Lunch Boxes featured in the book. The lunch boxes came in all shapes, sizes and colors.

Dedication

To my loving wife, Patty, without her love and support, none of this would have been possible. To all our old and new friends who helped us struggle to publish our first book ("Pictorial Price Guide to Metal Lunch Boxes & Thermoses"). All of you know what a labor of love this is and we hope it helps both newcomers and old timers enjoy the collecting of lunch boxes.

The Pricing

The values in this book should only be used as a guide. They are not intended to set prices which vary due to local demand, condition and availability. Auction and dealer prices also vary greatly. Neither the author nor the publisher assumes responsibility for any losses that might be incurred as a result of consulting this guide.

Acknowledgements

Our thanks to the following people who donated Lunch Boxes and time and friendship for our use in this book:

      Deb & Dan "The Massachusetts Boxers" Kozikowski
      Lee "The Thermos Man" Leonard
      Jerry "The Boxing Poet" Goebert
      Shawn "The Plastic Boxer" Osburn
      Joe & Lois "The Mint Boxers" Soucy
      Eric "The PA Thermos King" Haag
      Melanie & Jon "The Brooklyn Boxers" Shapiro
      Joseph "Underdog" Truitt
      Laszlo "The Rare Dome Boxer" Ficsor
      Terry "Lafayette Boxer" Vandervate
      Bob & Christine "Wordsmiths" Welter
      Mark "Gimme Dat Box" Blondy

Many thanks to all our collector friends and dealers from coast to coast that have traded and bought Lunch Boxes and Thermoses with me. This book would not have been possible without your help.

<u>Last, but not least, we would like to thank our families:</u>
      To Genell Kelley and Karlene and Noel Kelley, our love and thanks for your hospitality for putting up with us every Canton Weekend over the last few years. We really appreciate it. To our sons, Larry and Mike for their help and encouragement. A special thanks to Larry's Mom and Dad for their love, encouragement and always being there. To our two Special Sunrises in our lives, our granddaughters, Tiffany and Cassie, for believing we are perfect.

INTRODUCTION

In compiling material for The Pictorial Price Guide to Metal Lunch Boxes and Thermoses, 1992, we found we had too much material for the price range we wanted to publish. In order to make the material accessible to everyone, we divided the material. This book gives only a sample of some of the different vinyl & plastic lunch boxes that were manufactured.

This book focuses on the vinyl & plastic lunch boxes which obtained their highest popularity during the late 1960s and early 1970s.

The earliest vinyls were produced in the late 1940s and were styled as a vinyl bag with drawstrings. These were not widely popular and changed shape as the metal lunch boxes took off. When television produced a boom in heroes in the late 1950s manufacturers started producing the square vinyl lunch boxes. Not only to imitate the metal lunch boxes success, but also to overcome their drawbacks. Vinyl wouldn't rust and was flexible enough to resist denting. The industry came full circle when zippered, purselike vinyl brunch bags were introduced in the early 1960s.

Plastic lunch boxes were manufactured in the early 1960s and are still being produced today. Plastic and it's mold ability allowed manufacturers to produce lunch boxes in every shape imaginable - from cars to pickles.

The early vinyls with illustrations are very collectible and the hardest to find. Very often, after multiple washings the cardboard liner behind the vinyl would get wet, wrinkle and mom would toss it in favor of the newest and largest hero.

Subject material could be as simple as a lamb or a horse, a musical group or a movie theme. Boy and girl themes were very common.

Some "puffy" vinyls are included in this value guide. The style is often a product orientated "beverage cooler" rather than functioning specifically as lunch containers.

Whatever you enjoy collecting and whether or not it is for the thrill of the hunt, the investment possibilities or just to have something unique from your childhood, lunch box collecting will continue to appeal to those with a smile in their ages and fun in their heart.

Taking Care of Your Lunch Box Collection

Lunch Boxes are rare collectibles with limited availability for all who want them.

It is recommended that special care be taken in the storage and cleaning of your collection.

Harsh chemicals such as lighter fluid, paint thinners and even household cleaners, (such as ammonia based or alcohol based products) and paper towels can damage the pictures. Protect your investment!

Over time, I have developed a cleaning kit that removes dirt, rust, some markers, ink, tape stickers and sticker glue. At the same time, a protective non-yellowing wax is applied which helps to beautify and protect the surface of your Lunch Box. This one step process works on metal, vinyl, and plastic lunch boxes. The pictures in this book show you what you can do!!

The cleaning kit contains one 8 oz. bottle of cleaner (enough for 25-40 Lunch Boxes), soft cleaning cloth and easy to follow instructions. Order a cleaning kit for $9.95 plus $2.00 shipping and handling. Texas residents include 8.25% sales tax. Delivery within Continental United States. Elsewhere a higher shipping cost - write for details. Price subject to change with notice. 10 - 14 days shipping.

Order yours today and restore your collection.

Write to:
> Larry Aikins
> Rt. 5, Box 5174
> Athens, TX 75751
> Ph. (903) 675-3765

Lunch Box Convention

For the past 6 years Sandy and Bill Henry and his parents Billie and Bill Henry Sr., through much hard work and dedication, have put together the National Lunch Box Convention in Tennessee. Their kindness and hospitality are greatly appreciated by all that have attended and participated in the show. Since the first convention, lunch box collectors from all over the country have been coming together as a family.

Seeing old friends and meeting new ones. Telling stories of their adventures and sometime humorous hunts for the great elusive lunch box. Sharing with other collectors their favorite or most unique lunch box they have in their collection.

The buying, selling and trading that goes on during the two day convention are exciting to watch and participate in. The auction is an event not to be missed! If you are a lunch box enthusiast, you will not want to miss the next convention.

For more information, send a large stamped, self addressed envelope to Bill Henry, 104 Davidson Lane, Oakridge, Tennessee, 37830 or Larry Aikins, Rt. 5 - Box 5174, Athens, TX, 75751, Ph. (903) 675-3765.

Hope to see you there!!

Happy Boxing!

TABLE OF CONTENTS

Acknowledgements .... A
Introduction .... B
Taking Care of Your Lunch Box Collection C
Lunch Box Convention .... D
Table of Contents .... E
Advertising .... F
Vinyl Lunch Boxes & Thermoses .... 1 - 35
Plastic Lunch Boxes & Thermoses .... 36 - 89
Brunch Bags & Thermoses .... 90 - 104
Draw Strings & Thermoses .... 105 - 106
Extra Thermoses 107
Minis 108
Ceramic Lunch Boxes 109
How to Use Index, Price Guide & Inventory 110
Grading Your Lunch Boxes & Thermoses 111
Abbreviations for Manufacturers .... 112 - 113
Vinyl's Index & Price Guide .... 114 - 127
Plastic's Index & Price Guide .... 128 - 149
Brunch Bag's Index & Price Guide .... 150 - 155
Draw String's Index & Price Guide 156
Extra Thermose's Index & Price Guide 157
Mini's Index & Price Guide 158
Ceramic's Index & Price Guide 159

Vinyl Lunch Boxes

1

2

3

4

5

6

7

8

9

10

11

12

13

14

15

16

17

18

19

20

21

22

23

24

25

26

27

28

29

30

5

31

32

33

34

35

36

37

38

39

40

41

42

43

44

45

46

47

48

49

50

51

52

53

54

55

56

57

58

59

60

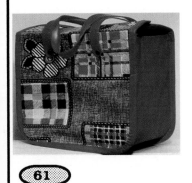

61

62

63

64

65

66

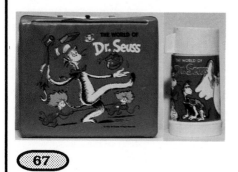

67

68

69

70

71

72

73

74

75

76

77

78

79

80

81

82

83

84

14

85

86

87

88

89

90

91

92

93

94

95

96

97

98

99

100

101

102

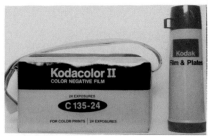

103

104

105

106

107

108

109

110

111

112

113

114

115

116

117

118

119

120

121

122

123

124

125

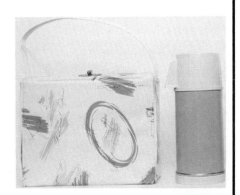

126

127

128

129

130

131

132

133

134

135

136

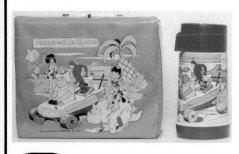

137

138

139

140

141

142

143

144

145

146

147

148

149

150

151

152

153

154

155

156

157

158

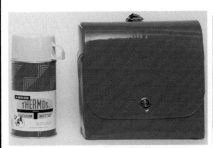

159

160

161

162

163

164

165

166

167

168

169

170

171

172

173

174

175

176

177

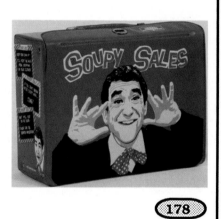

178

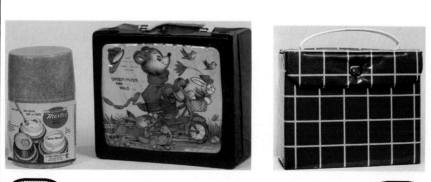

179

180

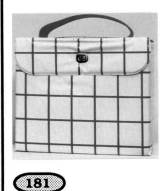

181

182

183

184

185

186

31

187

188

189

190

191

192

193

194

195

196

197

198

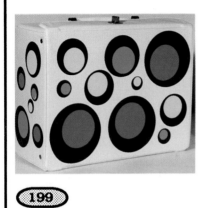

199

200

201

202

203

204

205

206

Plastic Lunch Boxes

1

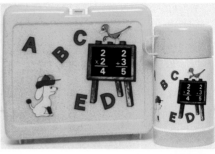

2

3

4

5

6

7

8

9

10

11

12

13

14

15

16

17

18

19

20

21

22

23

24

25

26

27

28

29

30

31

32

33

34

35

36

37

38

39

40

41

42

43

44

45

46

47

48

49

50

51

52

53

54

44

55

56

57

58

59

60

45

61

62

63

64

65

66

67

68

69

70

71

72

73

74

75

76

77

78

79

80

81

82

83

84

85

86

87

88

89

90

91

92

93

94

95

96

97

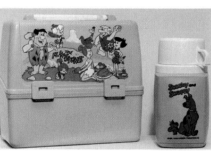

98

99

100

101

102

103

104

105

106

107

108

109

110

111

112

113

114

115

116

117

118

119

120

121

122

123

124

125

126

127

128

129

130

131

132

139

140

141

142

143

144

145

146

147

148

149

150

151

152

153

154

155

156

157

158

159

160

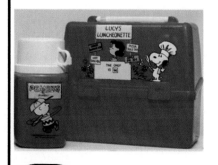

161

162

163

164

165

166

167

168

63

169

170

171

172

173

174

175

176

177

178

179

180

181

182

183

184

185

186

187

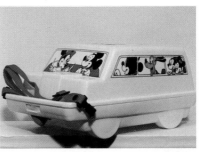

188

189

190

191

192

193

194

195

196

197

198

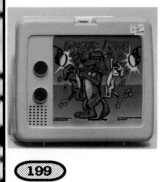

199

AM RADIO
LUNCHBOX
HEADPHONES/THERMO INCL.

200

201

202

203

MUPPET SCHOOL BUS

204

205

206

207

208

209

210

211

212

213

214

215

216

217

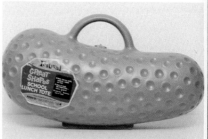

218

219

220

221

222

72

223

224

225

226

227

228

229

230

231

232

233

234

235

236

237

238

239

240

241

242

243

244

245

246

247

248

249

250

251

252

253

254

255

256

257

258

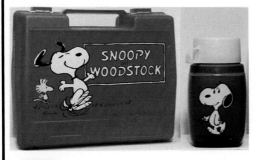

259

260

261

262

263

264

265

266

267

268

269

270

271

272

273

274

275

276

277

278

279

280

281

282

283

284

285

286

287

288

289

290

291

292

293

294

295

296

297

298

299

300

301

302

303

304

305

306

307

308

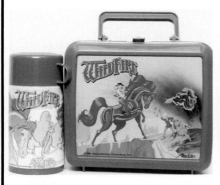

309

310

311

312

313

314

315

316

317

318

319

320

321

322

Brunch Bags

1

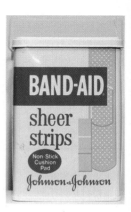

2

3

4

5

6

7

8

9

10

11

12

91

13

14

15

16

17

18

19

20

21

22

23

24

25

26

27

28

29

30

31

32

No Photo Available

No Photo Available

33

34

35

36

37

38

39

40

41

42

43

44

45

46

47

48

49

50

51

52

53

54

55

56

57

58

59

60

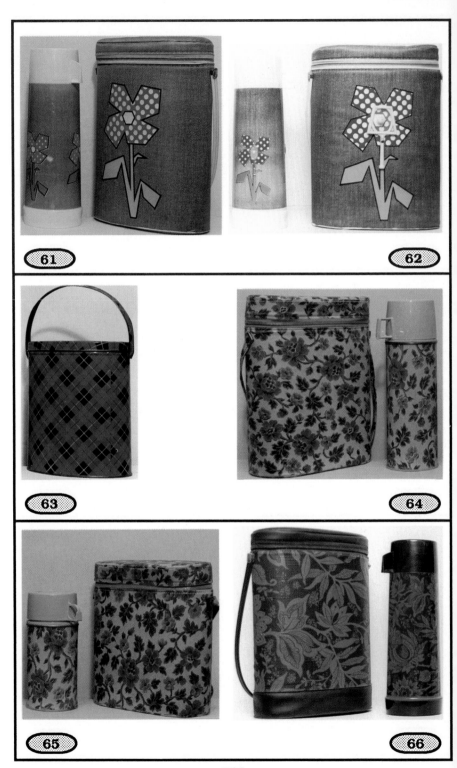

61

62

63

64

65

66

67

68

69

70

71

72

73

74

75

76

77

78

79

80

81

82

83

84

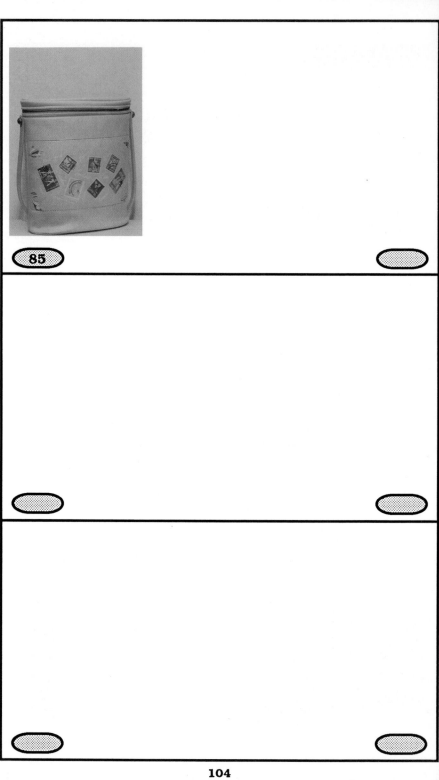

85

1

2

3

4

5

6

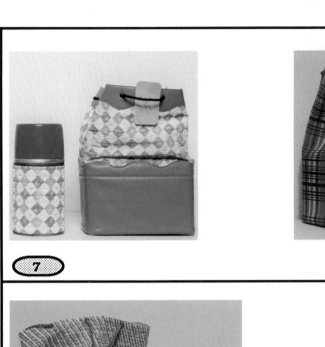

7

8

9

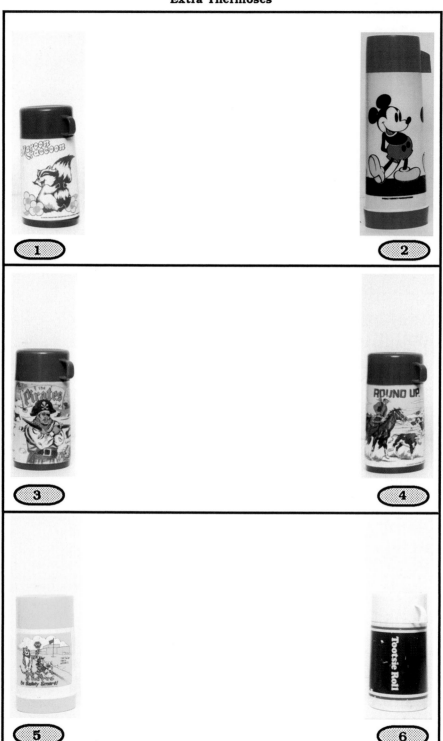

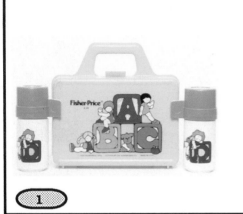

1

2

3

4

5

6

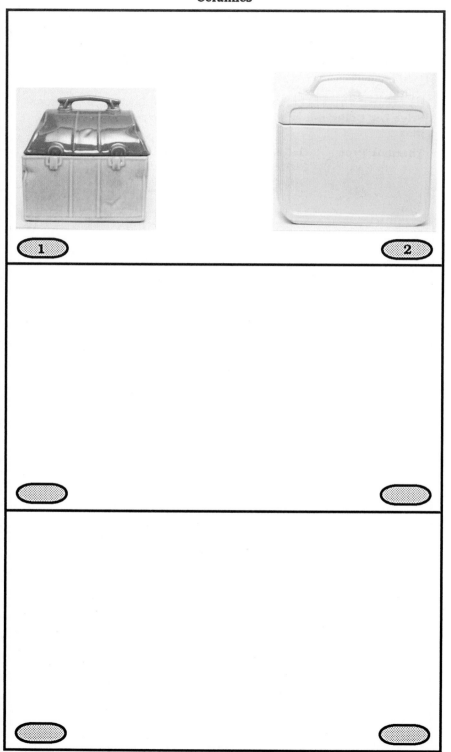

1

2

HOW TO USE THE COLLECTOR'S
INDEX, PRICE GUIDE AND INVENTORY PAGE

Item # is the number of kit in book.

$$ Column - Top is Lunch Box Current Value, Bottom is Thermos Price Log Column-how much collector has invested in kit & thermos

Thermos Type -   G=Generic   M=Matching
                 S=Steel   P=Plastic
                 S/G=Steel & Glass SYO=Styrofoam

Price Log

Item # - Name of Lunch Box	$$	Condition Lunch Box	
Year Maker Thermos Type	$$	Condition Thermos	

*** Current Values of Boxes and Thermoses are based on Excellent (Grade 8) condition.

SAMPLE BELOW:

Collector has Apple (Cube) in a grade 8 box with his cost at $30.
He has the Apple (Cube) thermos in a grade 6 with his cost at $10.
He has #10 Bach's Lunch box and thermos both grade 9, total cost $125.
He has no #11 Bach's Lunch box or thermos.
#13 Ballerina did not come with thermos.

Item	$$	Condition	Log
9 - Apple (Cube)	40	5̶ 6̶ 7̶ 8̶ 9 10	$30
87 UNK M/P	25	5̶ 6 7 8 9 10	$10
10 - Bach's Lunch	140	5̶ 6̶ 7̶ 8̶ 9̶ 10	$125
75 UNK SYO	12	5̶ 6̶ 7̶ 8̶ 9̶ 10	total
11 - Bach's Lunch	150	5 6 7 8 9 10	
VBI SYO	12	5 6 7 8 9 10	
12 - Ballerina	325	5̶ 6̶ 7̶ 8̶ 9̶ 1̶0̶	$320
62 AL M-S/G	110	5̶ 6̶ 7̶ 8̶ 9̶ 1̶0̶	$100
13 - Ballerina	120	5̶ 6̶ 7̶ 8 9 10	$60
60's AR		5 6 7 8 9 10	

Grading Your Lunch Boxes & Thermoses
Plastics

Grade

Poor	<u>5</u> - Missing handle or latch. Very bad breaks in plastic. Most of the decal is missing. Extra art work added with felt marker by child.
Good	<u>6</u> - Has small breaks or cracks in plastic. Small amounts of decal missing, wrinkling or bubbling of decal.
Fine	<u>7</u> - Has Bad scratches and wear on back and front. Decal has peeling around edges or starting to wrinkle or bubble.
Excellent	<u>8</u> - Scratches and wear on back and sides, but picture graphics are not damaged.
Near Mint	<u>9</u> - Looks new but shows signs of very little use, with very small hairline scratches on back.
Mint	<u>10</u> - Store stock new with original price tags.

**Plastic Boxes were made by injecting plastic into molds.

Grading Your Lunch Boxes & Thermoses
Vinyls

Grade

Poor	<u>5</u> - Missing handle or latch. Box will not hold it's shape, very bad splits all around edges. Hinge broken and bad felt marker marks or holes in vinyl.
Good	<u>6</u> - Box has lost shape due to water damage. Serious seam splitting. Broken hinges, handle or latch. Coming apart at the rivets and fading of vinyl.
Fine	<u>7</u> - Box has begun to lose it's shape. Splits up to 1" long at hinge, seam, around lid or front. Has felt marks and (or) bad rust on the closure.
Excellent	<u>8</u> - Shows normal wear on bottom and back. Kit holding it's shape with no bulging. Brass has tarnish. Vinyl starting to split on hinge.
Near Mint	<u>9</u> - Looks new, but shows signs of very little use. Very little tarnish on brass closure and rivets.
Mint	<u>10</u> - Store stock new with original price tags.

**Vinyls were made of cardboard covered with a shower curtain type vinyl for the cover.

Abbreviations for Manufacturers

AD - Adco Liberty
AL - Aladdin Industries
ALC - Aladdin Industries, Canada
ALH - Alladin Industries, Hallmark
ALV - Aladdin Industries, Venezuela
AR - Ardee
AT - American Thermos
AV - Avon
BA - Babcock
BB - Benrose, Brazil
BR - Brazil
BV - Bayville
CA - Canadian
CC - Continental Can
CH - China
CIM - Cipsa, Mexico
DA - Dart
DAS - D.A.S.
DCT - Deco, Taiwan
DE - Deka
EN - England
FD - Fun Design
FE - Feldco
FP - Fisher Price
FS - Fesco
FU - Fundes
G - Generic
GA - Gary
HB - Hasbro
HBT - Hanna Barbera Productions, Taiwan
HT - Holtemp
HU - Hummer
IS - Israel
IT - Italy

Abbreviations for Manufacturers

JA - Japan
K - Kruger
KST - King Seeley Thermos
ME - Mexico
MK - Metrokane
NE - Neevel
OA - Ohio Art
OC - Outer Circle
OK - Okay Industries
PP - Prepac
SDT - Selandia Designs, Taiwan
SE - Servo
SU - Superseal
TA - Taiwan
TB - Termolar, Brazil
TH - Thermos
THC - Thermos, Canada
THE - Thermos, England
TR - Traffic
TU - Tupperware
UK - United Kingdom
UN - Universal
UNK - Unknown
VBI - Volkwein Bros. Inc.

* Thermos is Corsage (#76 from Pictorial Price Guide to Metal Lunch Boxes and Thermoses).
** Thermos is Satellite (#343 from Pictorial Price Guide to Metal Lunch Boxes and Thermoses).
*** Makers Gary & Bayville's lunch boxes came in six different colors.
**** Maker Ardee's lunch boxes came in several different colors.

1 - Airline Stewardess	140	5	6	7	8	9	10	
72 AR SYO	20	5	6	7	8	9	10	
2 - Airport	145	5	6	7	8	9	10	
72 AR SYO	20	5	6	7	8	9	10	
3 - Alice In Wonderland	230	5	6	7	8	9	10	
74 AL M-P	45	5	6	7	8	9	10	
4 - All American	160	5	6	7	8	9	10	
76 BV SYO	20	5	6	7	8	9	10	
5 - All Dressed Up	90	5	6	7	8	9	10	
70's BV SYO	20	5	6	7	8	9	10	
6 - All Dressed Up	90	5	6	7	8	9	10	
70's BV SYO	20	5	6	7	8	9	10	
7 - Alvin	400	5	6	7	8	9	10	
63 KST M-P	140	5	6	7	8	9	10	
8 - Annie	75	5	6	7	8	9	10	
81 AL M-P	20	5	6	7	8	9	10	
9 - Apple (Cube)	40	5	6	7	8	9	10	
87 UNK M-P	25	5	6	7	8	9	10	
10 - Bach's Lunch (Front Red)	140	5	6	7	8	9	10	
75 VBI SYO	20	5	6	7	8	9	10	
11 - Bach's Lunch (Back Blue)	140	5	6	7	8	9	10	
75 VBI SYO	20	5	6	7	8	9	10	
12 - Ballerina	325	5	6	7	8	9	10	
62 AL M-S/G	125	5	6	7	8	9	10	
13 - Ballet	800	5	6	7	8	9	10	
61 UN		5	6	7	8	9	10	
14 - Ballerina	120	5	6	7	8	9	10	
60's AR		5	6	7	8	9	10	
15 - Banana Splits	450	5	6	7	8	9	10	
69 KST M-S/G	150	5	6	7	8	9	10	

Item	Year / Code	Price	5	6	7	8	9	10
16 - Barbie & Francie		120	5	6	7	8	9	10
	65 KST M-S/G	65	5	6	7	8	9	10
17 - Barbie & Midge		110	5	6	7	8	9	10
	63 KST M-S/G	65	5	6	7	8	9	10
18 - Barbie & Midge		110	5	6	7	8	9	10
	65 KST M-S/G	55	5	6	7	8	9	10
19 - Barbie & Midge (Dome)		525	5	6	7	8	9	10
	64 KST M-S/G	80	5	6	7	8	9	10
20 - Barbie & Midge w/s.v. handle		140	5	6	7	8	9	10
	64 KST M-S/G	65	5	6	7	8	9	10
21 - Barbie (Softy)		45	5	6	7	8	9	10
	88 KST P	15	5	6	7	8	9	10
22 - Barbie Lunch Box Ponytail		750	5	6	7	8	9	10
	61 KST M-S/G	90	5	6	7	8	9	10
23 - Barbie Lunch Kit		225	5	6	7	8	9	10
	62 KST M-S/G	90	5	6	7	8	9	10
24 - Barbie, World of (Blue)		90	5	6	7	8	9	10
	71 KST M-S/G	25	5	6	7	8	9	10
25 - Barbie, World of (Pink)		75	5	6	7	8	9	10
	71 KST M-S/G	25	5	6	7	8	9	10
26 - Barn (Dome)		125	5	6	7	8	9	10
	UNK		5	6	7	8	9	10
27 - Barn (Puffy)		90	5	6	7	8	9	10
	79 DA		5	6	7	8	9	10
28 - Barnum's Animals		60	5	6	7	8	9	10
	78 AD		5	6	7	8	9	10
29 - Batman (Softy)		65	5	6	7	8	9	10
	91 TH	20	5	6	7	8	9	10
30 - Beany & Cecil (Brown)		550	5	6	7	8	9	10
	63 KST M-S/G	150	5	6	7	8	9	10

31 - Beany & Cecil (White)	600	5 6 7 8 9 10	
62 KST M-S/G	150	5 6 7 8 9 10	
32 - Betsy Clark	140	5 6 7 8 9 10	
77 KST M-P	15	5 6 7 8 9 10	
33 - Black	45	5 6 7 8 9 10	
70 AL		5 6 7 8 9 10	
34 - Black (Dome)	110	5 6 7 8 9 10	
UNK		5 6 7 8 9 10	
35 - Boston Red Sox	90	5 6 7 8 9 10	
60's AR	20	5 6 7 8 9 10	
36 - Boy on Rocket	250	5 6 7 8 9 10	
60's UNK		5 6 7 8 9 10	
37 - Buick 1910	140	5 6 7 8 9 10	
74 BV SYO	20	5 6 7 8 9 10	
38 - Bullwinkle	450	5 6 7 8 9 10	
62 KST M-S/G	60	5 6 7 8 9 10	
39 - Captain Kangaroo	500	5 6 7 8 9 10	
64 UNK M-S/G	150	5 6 7 8 9 10	
40 - Cars	140	5 6 7 8 9 10	
60 AR		5 6 7 8 9 10	
41 - Care Bears	95	5 6 7 8 9 10	
80's ME		5 6 7 8 9 10	
42 - Carousel	425	5 6 7 8 9 10	
62 AL M-S/G	130	5 6 7 8 9 10	
43 - Casper	550	5 6 7 8 9 10	
66 KST M-S/G	150	5 6 7 8 9 10	
44 - Challenger (Puffy)	175	5 6 7 8 9 10	
86 BA		5 6 7 8 9 10	
45 - Circus (Softy)	45	5 6 7 8 9 10	
85 UNK		5 6 7 8 9 10	

46 - Circus Fun 60's UNK	110	5 6 7 8 9 10 5 6 7 8 9 10					
47 - Coca-Cola 80 AL SYO	160 20	5 6 7 8 9 10 5 6 7 8 9 10					
48 - Coco the Clown 70's GA SYO	110 20	5 6 7 8 9 10 5 6 7 8 9 10					
49 - Corsage 70 KST S/G	140 30	5 6 7 8 9 10 5 6 7 8 9 10					
50 - Cottage 74 KST	130	5 6 7 8 9 10 5 6 7 8 9 10					
51 - Crayon (Puffy) 84 UNK	40	5 6 7 8 9 10 5 6 7 8 9 10					
52 - Date Line (Beige Cube) 60's HB	140	5 6 7 8 9 10 5 6 7 8 9 10					
53 - Date Line (Blue Cube) 60's HB	140	5 6 7 8 9 10 5 6 7 8 9 10					
54 - Date Line (Blue) 60's HB	450	5 6 7 8 9 10 5 6 7 8 9 10					
55 - Date Line (Pink) 60's HB	450	5 6 7 8 9 10 5 6 7 8 9 10					
56 - Dawn 72 AL M-P	140 35	5 6 7 8 9 10 5 6 7 8 9 10					
57 - Dawn 71 AL M-P	140 35	5 6 7 8 9 10 5 6 7 8 9 10					
58 - Dear God Kids 86 BB	85	5 6 7 8 9 10 5 6 7 8 9 10					
59 - Deer 60's UNK	250	5 6 7 8 9 10 5 6 7 8 9 10					
60 - Denim 70's KST M-S/G	50 20	5 6 7 8 9 10 5 6 7 8 9 10					

61 - Denim & Red	25	5	6	7	8	9	10	
UNK		5	6	7	8	9	10	
62 - Denim w/flowers	45	5	6	7	8	9	10	
84 UNK		5	6	7	8	9	10	
63 - Deputy Dawg	550	5	6	7	8	9	10	
64 TH		5	6	7	8	9	10	
64 - Dog House	165	5	6	7	8	9	10	
74 TB M-P	40	5	6	7	8	9	10	
65 - Donny & Marie	110	5	6	7	8	9	10	
76 AL M-P	20	5	6	7	8	9	10	
66 - Donny & Marie	120	5	6	7	8	9	10	
78 AL M-P	20	5	6	7	8	9	10	
67 - Dr. Seuss	570	5	6	7	8	9	10	
70 AL M-P	60	5	6	7	8	9	10	
68 - Dream Boat	840	5	6	7	8	9	10	
60 FE SYO	15	5	6	7	8	9	10	
69 - Dudley Do-Right	1500	5	6	7	8	9	10	
AR		5	6	7	8	9	10	
70 - Engine Co. No. 1	120	5	6	7	8	9	10	
74 DA		5	6	7	8	9	10	
71 - European Map (Dome)	240	5	6	7	8	9	10	
UNK		5	6	7	8	9	10	
72 - Fawn	140	5	6	7	8	9	10	
60's UNK		5	6	7	8	9	10	
73 - Fess Parker	325	5	6	7	8	9	10	
60's AL		5	6	7	8	9	10	
74 - Fire Dept. (Softy)	110	5	6	7	8	9	10	
UNK		5	6	7	8	9	10	
75 - Fishing	160	5	6	7	8	9	10	
70 AR SYO	20	5	6	7	8	9	10	

76 - Freihofer's Cookies 60's UNK	120	5 6 7 8 9 10 5 6 7 8 9 10						
77 - Frog Flutist 75 AL M-P	75 25	5 6 7 8 9 10 5 6 7 8 9 10						
78 - G.I. Joe 89 KST G-P	55 10	5 6 7 8 9 10 5 6 7 8 9 10						
79 - G.I. Joe UNK SYO	270 20	5 6 7 8 9 10 5 6 7 8 9 10						
80 - Garfield 78 ME	150	5 6 7 8 9 10 5 6 7 8 9 10						
81 - Gigi 62 AL M-S/G	280 80	5 6 7 8 9 10 5 6 7 8 9 10						
82 - Girl & Poodle 60 AR SYO	140 20	5 6 7 8 9 10 5 6 7 8 9 10						
83 - Go Go 66 AL M-S/G	190 90	5 6 7 8 9 10 5 6 7 8 9 10						
84 - Goat Butt 65 AR SYO	160 20	5 6 7 8 9 10 5 6 7 8 9 10						
85 - Goat Butt 65 AR SYO	160 20	5 6 7 8 9 10 5 6 7 8 9 10						
86 - Goodie Box 60 UNK	140	5 6 7 8 9 10 5 6 7 8 9 10						
87 - Gray (Dome) UNK	125	5 6 7 8 9 10 5 6 7 8 9 10						
88 - Happy Powwow 70's BV SYO	110 20	5 6 7 8 9 10 5 6 7 8 9 10						
89 - Happy Powwow 70's BV SYO	110 20	5 6 7 8 9 10 5 6 7 8 9 10						
90 - Haunted House 79 DA	85	5 6 7 8 9 10 5 6 7 8 9 10						

91 - Highway Sign's Snap Pack 88 AV	40	5 6 7 8 9 10 5 6 7 8 9 10						
92 - Holly Hobbie 72 AL M-P	45 15	5 6 7 8 9 10 5 6 7 8 9 10						
93 - I Love a Parade 70 BV SYO	130 20	5 6 7 8 9 10 5 6 7 8 9 10						
94 - Ice Cream (Pink Gingham) 75 AL M-P	55 25	5 6 7 8 9 10 5 6 7 8 9 10						
95 - Indian Kids (Dome) CA	180	5 6 7 8 9 10 5 6 7 8 9 10						
96 - It's a Small World 68 AL M-S/G	250 110	5 6 7 8 9 10 5 6 7 8 9 10						
97 - Jonathan Livingston Seagull 74 AL M-P	160 35	5 6 7 8 9 10 5 6 7 8 9 10						
98 - Jr. Miss Safari 62 PP	140	5 6 7 8 9 10 5 6 7 8 9 10						
99 - Junior Deb 60 AL M-S/G	175 55	5 6 7 8 9 10 5 6 7 8 9 10						
100 - Junior Nurse 63 KST M-S/G	320 90	5 6 7 8 9 10 5 6 7 8 9 10						
101 - Kaboodle Kit (Pink) 60's AL	160	5 6 7 8 9 10 5 6 7 8 9 10						
102 - Kaboodle Kit (White) 60's AL	160	5 6 7 8 9 10 5 6 7 8 9 10						
103 - Kodak Gold 70's AL	85 20	5 6 7 8 9 10 5 6 7 8 9 10						
104 - Kodak II 70's AL	95 20	5 6 7 8 9 10 5 6 7 8 9 10						
105 - L'il Jodie (Puffy) 85 BA	90	5 6 7 8 9 10 5 6 7 8 9 10						

106 - Lassie	120	5	6	7	8	9	10	
60's AR SYO	20	5	6	7	8	9	10	
107 - Liddle Kiddles	250	5	6	7	8	9	10	
69 KST M-S/G	60	5	6	7	8	9	10	
108 - Linus! The Lion Hearted	550	5	6	7	8	9	10	
65 AL M-S	110	5	6	7	8	9	10	
109 - Lion (Puffy)	60	5	6	7	8	9	10	
85 BA		5	6	7	8	9	10	
110 - Lion in Van	145	5	6	7	8	9	10	
78 KST		5	6	7	8	9	10	
111 - Liquor Labels	310	5	6	7	8	9	10	
UNK		5	6	7	8	9	10	
112 - Little Ballerina	75	5	6	7	8	9	10	
75 BV SYO	20	5	6	7	8	9	10	
113 - Little Old Schoolhouse	80	5	6	7	8	9	10	
74 DA		5	6	7	8	9	10	
114 - Love	160	5	6	7	8	9	10	
72 AL M-P	45	5	6	7	8	9	10	
115 - Lunch 'n Munch	675	5	6	7	8	9	10	
59 AT *	70	5	6	7	8	9	10	
116 - Mam'zelle	180	5	6	7	8	9	10	
71 AL M-P	65	5	6	7	8	9	10	
117 - Mardi-gras	80	5	6	7	8	9	10	
71 AL M-P	20	5	6	7	8	9	10	
118 - Mary Ann	75	5	6	7	8	9	10	
60 AL M-S/G	25	5	6	7	8	9	10	
119 - Mary Poppins	140	5	6	7	8	9	10	
73 AL M-P	50	5	6	7	8	9	10	
120 - Mickey Mouse	120	5	6	7	8	9	10	
ME		5	6	7	8	9	10	

121 - Mickey Mouse Kaboodle Kit	325	5 6 7 8 9 10	
63 UNK		5 6 7 8 9 10	
122 - Monkees	380	5 6 7 8 9 10	
67 KST M-S/G	125	5 6 7 8 9 10	
123 - Mr. Peanut Snap Pack	110	5 6 7 8 9 10	
79 DA		5 6 7 8 9 10	
124 - Mushrooms	125	5 6 7 8 9 10	
72 AL M-P	45	5 6 7 8 9 10	
125 - My Cookie Carrier	85	5 6 7 8 9 10	
G		5 6 7 8 9 10	
126 - National Open	180	5 6 7 8 9 10	
60's UN S/G	45	5 6 7 8 9 10	
127 - New Zoo Revue	210	5 6 7 8 9 10	
70's AL M-P	55	5 6 7 8 9 10	
128 - Nickelodeon	90	5 6 7 8 9 10	
G		5 6 7 8 9 10	
129 - Ogilvy & Mather	60	5 6 7 8 9 10	
G		5 6 7 8 9 10	
130 - Our Song	250	5 6 7 8 9 10	
60's UNK		5 6 7 8 9 10	
131 - Pac-Man (Puffy)	65	5 6 7 8 9 10	
85 AL		5 6 7 8 9 10	
132 - Peanuts (Green)	150	5 6 7 8 9 10	
71 KST S/G	30	5 6 7 8 9 10	
133 - Peanuts (Red)	90	5 6 7 8 9 10	
67 KST M-S/G	30	5 6 7 8 9 10	
134 - Peanuts (Red)	90	5 6 7 8 9 10	
69 KST S/G	30	5 6 7 8 9 10	
135 - Peanuts (Red)	130	5 6 7 8 9 10	
KST S/G	30	5 6 7 8 9 10	

136 - Peanuts (White)	90	5 6 7 8 9 10	
73 KST S/G	30	5 6 7 8 9 10	
137 - Pebbles & Bamm-Bamm	250	5 6 7 8 9 10	
78 GA M-P	55	5 6 7 8 9 10	
138 - Penelope & Penny	120	5 6 7 8 9 10	
70's GA SYO	20	5 6 7 8 9 10	
139 - Penelope & Penny	120	5 6 7 8 9 10	
70's GA SYO	20	5 6 7 8 9 10	
140 - Peter Pan	210	5 6 7 8 9 10	
69 AL M-P	65	5 6 7 8 9 10	
141 - Peter Pan Peanut Butter (Cube)	130	5 6 7 8 9 10	
UNK		5 6 7 8 9 10	
142 - Picadilly	85	5 6 7 8 9 10	
71 AL M-P	20	5 6 7 8 9 10	
143 - Pink Panther	95	5 6 7 8 9 10	
80 AL M-P	20	5 6 7 8 9 10	
144 - Pique	125	5 6 7 8 9 10	
85 ME		5 6 7 8 9 10	
145 - Pony Tail	185	5 6 7 8 9 10	
60 KST S/G**	40	5 6 7 8 9 10	
146 - Pony Tail	450	5 6 7 8 9 10	
65 KST S/G**	40	5 6 7 8 9 10	
147 - Pony Tail Tid-Bit-Kit	260	5 6 7 8 9 10	
62 KST S/G**	40	5 6 7 8 9 10	
148 - Pony Tail Tid-Bit-Kit	175	5 6 7 8 9 10	
60's TH		5 6 7 8 9 10	
149 - Pony Tail Tid-Bit-Kit	225	5 6 7 8 9 10	
62 TH	40	5 6 7 8 9 10	
150 - Pony Tail w/Gray Border	220	5 6 7 8 9 10	
60's TH		5 6 7 8 9 10	

151 - Princess	180	5	6	7	8	9	10	
63 AL M-S/G	55	5	6	7	8	9	10	
152 - Psychedelic	150	5	6	7	8	9	10	
60's UNK		5	6	7	8	9	10	
153 - Psychedelic (Blue)	70	5	6	7	8	9	10	
70 KST M-S/G	30	5	6	7	8	9	10	
154 - Psychedelic (Yellow)	130	5	6	7	8	9	10	
69 AL M-S/G	60	5	6	7	8	9	10	
155 - Pussycats	220	5	6	7	8	9	10	
68 AL	80	5	6	7	8	9	10	
156 - Quilt Work (Dome)	145	5	6	7	8	9	10	
UNK		5	6	7	8	9	10	
157 - Race Car (Puffy)	45	5	6	7	8	9	10	
UNK		5	6	7	8	9	10	
158 - Raggedy Ann & Andy	110	5	6	7	8	9	10	
77 AL M-P	35	5	6	7	8	9	10	
159 - Red (Dome)	125	5	6	7	8	9	10	
60's TH	20	5	6	7	8	9	10	
160 - Ringling Bros.	325	5	6	7	8	9	10	
70 KST M-S/G	140	5	6	7	8	9	10	
161 - Ringling Bros. & Barnum	110	5	6	7	8	9	10	
80's UNK		5	6	7	8	9	10	
162 - Road Tote (Red)	250	5	6	7	8	9	10	
UNK		5	6	7	8	9	10	
163 - Road Tote (Yellow)	225	5	6	7	8	9	10	
UNK		5	6	7	8	9	10	
164 - Roy Rogers (Brown)	225	5	6	7	8	9	10	
60 KST S/G	95	5	6	7	8	9	10	
165 - Roy Rogers (Cream)	650	5	6	7	8	9	10	
60 KST S/G	95	5	6	7	8	9	10	

166 - Sabrina	230	5	6	7	8	9	10	
72 AL M-P	85	5	6	7	8	9	10	
167 - School Bus (Puffy)	45	5	6	7	8	9	10	
85 UNK		5	6	7	8	9	10	
168 - Sesame Street	85	5	6	7	8	9	10	
79 AL M-P	15	5	6	7	8	9	10	
169 - Sesame Street	60	5	6	7	8	9	10	
81 AL M-P	15	5	6	7	8	9	10	
170 - Shari Lewis	470	5	6	7	8	9	10	
63 AL M-S/G	120	5	6	7	8	9	10	
171 - Sizzlers	225	5	6	7	8	9	10	
71 KST S/G	60	5	6	7	8	9	10	
172 - Skipper	220	5	6	7	8	9	10	
65 KST S/G	60	5	6	7	8	9	10	
173 - Sleeping Beauty	240	5	6	7	8	9	10	
70 AL M-P	80	5	6	7	8	9	10	
174 - Snoopy (Softy)	45	5	6	7	8	9	10	
88 KST M-P	12	5	6	7	8	9	10	
175 - Snow White	285	5	6	7	8	9	10	
67 UNK		5	6	7	8	9	10	
176 - Snow White	220	5	6	7	8	9	10	
75 AL M-P	45	5	6	7	8	9	10	
177 - Soda	160	5	6	7	8	9	10	
60's UNK		5	6	7	8	9	10	
178 - Soupy Sales	475	5	6	7	8	9	10	
66 KST		5	6	7	8	9	10	
179 - Speedy Petey & Pals	140	5	6	7	8	9	10	
GA	20	5	6	7	8	9	10	
180 - Squares (Blue)	60	5	6	7	8	9	10	
UNK		5	6	7	8	9	10	

181 - Squares (White)	60	5	6	7	8	9	10	
UNK		5	6	7	8	9	10	
182 - Stardome	50	5	6	7	8	9	10	
UNK		5	6	7	8	9	10	
183 - Strawberry Shortcake	40	5	6	7	8	9	10	
80　AL　M-P	15	5	6	7	8	9	10	
184 - Sunset Snap Pack	60	5	6	7	8	9	10	
79　DA		5	6	7	8	9	10	
185 - Tammy	240	5	6	7	8	9	10	
64　AL　M-S/G	85	5	6	7	8	9	10	
186 - Tammy & Pepper	240	5	6	7	8	9	10	
65　AL　M-S/G	85	5	6	7	8	9	10	
187 - Tan (Dome)	120	5	6	7	8	9	10	
UNK		5	6	7	8	9	10	
188 - Tic Tac Toe (Blue)	50	5	6	7	8	9	10	
UNK		5	6	7	8	9	10	
189 - Tic Tac Toe (Red)	50	5	6	7	8	9	10	
UNK		5	6	7	8	9	10	
190 - Tiger w/Umbrella	145	5	6	7	8	9	10	
NE　SYO	15	5	6	7	8	9	10	
191 - Tina Teen	260	5	6	7	8	9	10	
60's　UNK		5	6	7	8	9	10	
192 - Tinkerbell	260	5	6	7	8	9	10	
69　AL　M-P	90	5	6	7	8	9	10	
193 - Trans-Formers, The Movie	90	5	6	7	8	9	10	
86　G		5	6	7	8	9	10	
194 - Tropic Swim Club	65	5	6	7	8	9	10	
89　G		5	6	7	8	9	10	
195 - Tweed (Brown)	60	5	6	7	8	9	10	
G		5	6	7	8	9	10	

196 - Twiggy	220	5	6	7	8	9	10	
67 AL M-S/G	80	5	6	7	8	9	10	
197 - Underdog w/Sales Samples	1500	5	6	7	8	9	10	
70's AR	15	5	6	7	8	9	10	
*Bullwinkle (Sales sample came with Underdog)	250	5	6	7	8	9	10	
		5	6	7	8	9	10	
*Tennessee Tuxedo (Sales sample came with Underdog)	250	5	6	7	8	9	10	
		5	6	7	8	9	10	
*Dudley-Do-Right (Sales sample came with Underdog)	250	5	6	7	8	9	10	
		5	6	7	8	9	10	
*Underdog (Sales sample came with Underdog)	250	5	6	7	8	9	10	
		5	6	7	8	9	10	
198 - Washington Apple	35	5	6	7	8	9	10	
UNK		5	6	7	8	9	10	
199 - White Psychedelic	310	5	6	7	8	9	10	
62 TH		5	6	7	8	9	10	
200 - Wizard in Van	145	5	6	7	8	9	10	
78 KST		5	6	7	8	9	10	
201 - Wonder Woman (Blue)	150	5	6	7	8	9	10	
77 AL M-P	35	5	6	7	8	9	10	
202 - Wonder Woman (Yellow)	200	5	6	7	8	9	10	
78 AL M-P	35	5	6	7	8	9	10	
203 - Wrangler	325	5	6	7	8	9	10	
62 AL	95	5	6	7	8	9	10	
204 - Yellow	35	5	6	7	8	9	10	
UNK		5	6	7	8	9	10	
205 - Yosemite Sam	560	5	6	7	8	9	10	
71 KST M-S/G	140	5	6	7	8	9	10	
206 - Ziggy's	140	5	6	7	8	9	10	
79 AL M-P	40	5	6	7	8	9	10	

1 - 101 Dalmations	18	5	6	7	8	9	10	
90 AL M-P	8	5	6	7	8	9	10	
2 - ABC	12	5	6	7	8	9	10	
TA M-P	5	5	6	7	8	9	10	
3 - All Dogs go to Heaven	30	5	6	7	8	9	10	
89 UNK M-P	10	5	6	7	8	9	10	
4 - Alphabet Sandwich	15	5	6	7	8	9	10	
78 TU		5	6	7	8	9	10	
5 - Animal (Dome)	20	5	6	7	8	9	10	
90 TR		5	6	7	8	9	10	
6 - Animal Friends (Pat Wong)	25	5	6	7	8	9	10	
85 SDT M-P	15	5	6	7	8	9	10	
7 - Animalympics (Dome)	35	5	6	7	8	9	10	
79 TH M-P	10	5	6	7	8	9	10	
8 - Army Issue	20	5	6	7	8	9	10	
79 TA		5	6	7	8	9	10	
9 - Astrokids	30	5	6	7	8	9	10	
88 BR M-P	15	5	6	7	8	9	10	
10 - Astronauts	30	5	6	7	8	9	10	
86 TH M-P	15	5	6	7	8	9	10	
11 - Astros Orbit	40	5	6	7	8	9	10	
82 TA M-P	20	5	6	7	8	9	10	
12 - Atari Missle Command (Dome)	35	5	6	7	8	9	10	
83 AL M-P	10	5	6	7	8	9	10	
13 - Back to School	60	5	6	7	8	9	10	
80 AL M-P	20	5	6	7	8	9	10	
14 - Back to the Future	30	5	6	7	8	9	10	
89 TH M-P	12	5	6	7	8	9	10	
15 - Bang Bang	45	5	6	7	8	9	10	
82 TH M-P		5	6	7	8	9	10	

16 - Barbie w/Hologram Mirror	25	5 6 7 8 9 10	
90 TH M-P	8	5 6 7 8 9 10	
17 - Barnaby Bear w/Black Board	20	5 6 7 8 9 10	
87 UK		5 6 7 8 9 10	
18 - Batman (Black)	45	5 6 7 8 9 10	
89 TA M-P	20	5 6 7 8 9 10	
19 - Batman (Dark Blue)	20	5 6 7 8 9 10	
89 TH M-P	10	5 6 7 8 9 10	
20 - Batman (Light Blue)	40	5 6 7 8 9 10	
89 TH M-P	10	5 6 7 8 9 10	
21 - Batman Finished Art Work Decal	350	5 6 7 8 9 10	
85 TH		5 6 7 8 9 10	
22 - Batman Prototype Sales Sample	850	5 6 7 8 9 10	
85 TH M-P	300	5 6 7 8 9 10	
23 - Batman Returns	15	5 6 7 8 9 10	
91 TH M-P	5	5 6 7 8 9 10	
24 - Batman-no glove (D.Blue)	30	5 6 7 8 9 10	
89 TH M-P	10	5 6 7 8 9 10	
25 - Batman-no glove (Gray)	85	5 6 7 8 9 10	
89 TH M-P	10	5 6 7 8 9 10	
26 - Beach Bronto	50	5 6 7 8 9 10	
84 AL		5 6 7 8 9 10	
27 - Beach Party (Blue)	15	5 6 7 8 9 10	
88 DE G-P	5	5 6 7 8 9 10	
28 - Beach Party (Pink)	15	5 6 7 8 9 10	
88 DE G-P	5	5 6 7 8 9 10	
29 - Bear (Flat-Blue)	15	5 6 7 8 9 10	
88 TA G-P	5	5 6 7 8 9 10	
30 - Bear (Flat-Green)	15	5 6 7 8 9 10	
88 TA G-P	5	5 6 7 8 9 10	

31 - Bear Box **88 CIM**	10	5	6	7	8	9	10	
		5	6	7	8	9	10	
32 - Bear w/Heart (3-D) **87 SE**	12	5	6	7	8	9	10	
		5	6	7	8	9	10	
33 - Beauty & the Beast **91 AL M-P**	20	5	6	7	8	9	10	
	5	5	6	7	8	9	10	
34 - Bee Gees **78 TH M-P**	40	5	6	7	8	9	10	
	20	5	6	7	8	9	10	
35 - Beetlejuice **89 TH M-P**	15	5	6	7	8	9	10	
	5	5	6	7	8	9	10	
36 - Benji **80 TH M-P**	20	5	6	7	8	9	10	
	10	5	6	7	8	9	10	
37 - Big Jim **76 TH M-P**	80	5	6	7	8	9	10	
	30	5	6	7	8	9	10	
38 - Black Hole **78 ALC M-P**	60	5	6	7	8	9	10	
	30	5	6	7	8	9	10	
39 - Blue (Dome) **75 TH G-P**	20	5	6	7	8	9	10	
	5	5	6	7	8	9	10	
40 - Blue (Dome) **81 AL G-P**	20	5	6	7	8	9	10	
	12	5	6	7	8	9	10	
41 - BMX **78 ALV M-P**	40	5	6	7	8	9	10	
	20	5	6	7	8	9	10	
42 - Bobby Orr (Six Million Dollar Man) **74 ALC M-P**	150	5	6	7	8	9	10	
	70	5	6	7	8	9	10	
43 - Bozostuffs **88 DE M-P**	40	5	6	7	8	9	10	
	20	5	6	7	8	9	10	
44 - Bread Loaf **80 IT**	110	5	6	7	8	9	10	
		5	6	7	8	9	10	
45 - Burger King (Give Away) **TA**	8	5	6	7	8	9	10	
		5	6	7	8	9	10	

46 - C.B. Bears 77 TH	20 	5 6 7 8 9 10 5 6 7 8 9 10	
47 - Camera 86 TA G-P	40 5	5 6 7 8 9 10 5 6 7 8 9 10	
48 - Car (Blue) 80 TA G-P	15 5	5 6 7 8 9 10 5 6 7 8 9 10	
49 - Car (Red) 80 TA G-P	15 5	5 6 7 8 9 10 5 6 7 8 9 10	
50 - Car (White) 80 TA G-P	15 5	5 6 7 8 9 10 5 6 7 8 9 10	
51 - Car (Yellow) 80 TA G-P	15 5	5 6 7 8 9 10 5 6 7 8 9 10	
52 - Car w/Bears 85 TA G-P	15 5	5 6 7 8 9 10 5 6 7 8 9 10	
53 - Care Bears 86 AL M-P	10 4	5 6 7 8 9 10 5 6 7 8 9 10	
54 - Caution (I brake for recess) w/Radio 86 TA	45 	5 6 7 8 9 10 5 6 7 8 9 10	
55 - Centurions 86 TH M-P	15 8	5 6 7 8 9 10 5 6 7 8 9 10	
56 - Chavo 79 ALC M-P	60 25	5 6 7 8 9 10 5 6 7 8 9 10	
57 - Chiclets 87 TH	40 	5 6 7 8 9 10 5 6 7 8 9 10	
58 - Chip-A-Saurus (Cookies) TA	10 	5 6 7 8 9 10 5 6 7 8 9 10	
59 - Chipmunks 83 TH M-P	25 10	5 6 7 8 9 10 5 6 7 8 9 10	
60 - Chips (Dome) 77 TH M-P	45 15	5 6 7 8 9 10 5 6 7 8 9 10	

61 - Cinderella	25	5 6 7 8 9 10			
92 AL M-P	10	5 6 7 8 9 10			
62 - Click Case w/Space Decals	20	5 6 7 8 9 10			
88 OC		5 6 7 8 9 10			
63 - Coca-Cola	60	5 6 7 8 9 10			
85 CIM M-P	20	5 6 7 8 9 10			
64 - Coca-Cola in 9 Languages	50	5 6 7 8 9 10			
81 AL M-P	20	5 6 7 8 9 10			
65 - Crazy Shirts	20	5 6 7 8 9 10			
83 UNK		5 6 7 8 9 10			
66 - Curiosity Shop	45	5 6 7 8 9 10			
72 TH M-S/G	30	5 6 7 8 9 10			
67 - Dallas Cowboys NFL	25	5 6 7 8 9 10			
85 TA M-P	12	5 6 7 8 9 10			
68 - Days of Thunder	30	5 6 7 8 9 10			
88 TH M-P	10	5 6 7 8 9 10			
69 - Deka 4x4	25	5 6 7 8 9 10			
88 DE G-P	5	5 6 7 8 9 10			
70 - Dick Tracy	20	5 6 7 8 9 10			
89 AL M-P	10	5 6 7 8 9 10			
71 - Dino Rex	20	5 6 7 8 9 10			
DCT M-P	10	5 6 7 8 9 10			
72 - Dino Riders	20	5 6 7 8 9 10			
88 AL M-P	10	5 6 7 8 9 10			
73 - Dinobeasties	15	5 6 7 8 9 10			
88 TH		5 6 7 8 9 10			
74 - Dinorocker w/Radio & Headset	45	5 6 7 8 9 10			
86 FU		5 6 7 8 9 10			
75 - Dinosaur	20	5 6 7 8 9 10			
88 TA M-P	10	5 6 7 8 9 10			

76 - Disney World	40	5	6	7	8	9	10	
74 ALC M-P	10	5	6	7	8	9	10	
77 - Dog & Rabbit	20	5	6	7	8	9	10	
87 TA M-P	10	5	6	7	8	9	10	
78 - Double Canteen Jam Box	40	5	6	7	8	9	10	
75 CH	10	5	6	7	8	9	10	
79 - Dr. Pepper	70	5	6	7	8	9	10	
82 TA M-P	30	5	6	7	8	9	10	
80 - Droids Star Wars	50	5	6	7	8	9	10	
85 TH M-P	15	5	6	7	8	9	10	
81 - Duck Tales (4x4)	15	5	6	7	8	9	10	
86 AL M-P	8	5	6	7	8	9	10	
82 - Duck Tales (Game)	15	5	6	7	8	9	10	
86 AL M-P	8	5	6	7	8	9	10	
83 - Dukes of Hazzard	45	5	6	7	8	9	10	
81 AL M-P	15	5	6	7	8	9	10	
84 - Dukes of Hazzard (Dome)	45	5	6	7	8	9	10	
81 AL M-P	15	5	6	7	8	9	10	
85 - Dune	45	5	6	7	8	9	10	
84 AL M-P	20	5	6	7	8	9	10	
86 - Dunkin Munchkins	45	5	6	7	8	9	10	
72 TH M-P	25	5	6	7	8	9	10	
87 - Ecology (Dome)	45	5	6	7	8	9	10	
80 TH M-P	20	5	6	7	8	9	10	
88 - Ed Grimley	25	5	6	7	8	9	10	
88 AL M-P	10	5	6	7	8	9	10	
89 - Entenmann's	25	5	6	7	8	9	10	
89 TH		5	6	7	8	9	10	
90 - Ewoks	20	5	6	7	8	9	10	
83 TH M-P	10	5	6	7	8	9	10	

91 - Fame	35	5	6	7	8	9	10	
72 **TH** **M-P**	15	5	6	7	8	9	10	
92 - Fat Albert w/Giveaway Samples	40	5	6	7	8	9	10	
73 **TH** **M-P**	15	5	6	7	8	9	10	
93 - Fievel Goes West	10	5	6	7	8	9	10	
91 **AL** **M-P**	5	5	6	7	8	9	10	
94 - Fire Engine Co. 7	30	5	6	7	8	9	10	
85 **DAS** **G-P**	8	5	6	7	8	9	10	
95 - Flash Gordon (Dome)	75	5	6	7	8	9	10	
79 **AL** **M-P**	40	5	6	7	8	9	10	
96 - Flinstone Kids	40	5	6	7	8	9	10	
87 **TH** **M-P**	10	5	6	7	8	9	10	
97 - Flinstones (A day at the zoo)	45	5	6	7	8	9	10	
89 **TA** **M-P**	15	5	6	7	8	9	10	
98 - Flinstones-(F) (Dome), Scooby & Scrappy-(B)	45	5	6	7	8	9	10	
81 **TH** **M-P**	15	5	6	7	8	9	10	
99 - Flinstones (The Dinos)	40	5	6	7	8	9	10	
89 **TA** **M-P**	15	5	6	7	8	9	10	
100 - Flower Fairies w/Snakes & Ladders Game	25	5	6	7	8	9	10	
80 **THE** **M-P**	15	5	6	7	8	9	10	
101 - Food Fighters	20	5	6	7	8	9	10	
88 **AL** **M-P**	10	5	6	7	8	9	10	
102 - Fraggle Rock	15	5	6	7	8	9	10	
87 **TH** **M-P**	8	5	6	7	8	9	10	
103 - Frito Lay's	50	5	6	7	8	9	10	
82 **TH**		5	6	7	8	9	10	
104 - G.I. Joe	15	5	6	7	8	9	10	
86 **AL** **M-P**	8	5	6	7	8	9	10	
105 - G.I. Joe	25	5	6	7	8	9	10	
89 **AL** **M-P**	15	5	6	7	8	9	10	

106 - Garfield (Dome)	60	5	6	7	8	9	10	
78 THC G-P	15	5	6	7	8	9	10	
107 - Garfield (Food Fight)	25	5	6	7	8	9	10	
79 TH M-P	10	5	6	7	8	9	10	
108 - Garfield (Lunch)	25	5	6	7	8	9	10	
77 TH M-P	10	5	6	7	8	9	10	
109 - Garfield w/Snakes & Ladders Game	40	5	6	7	8	9	10	
80 THE		5	6	7	8	9	10	
110 - Geoffrey	30	5	6	7	8	9	10	
81 AL M-P	10	5	6	7	8	9	10	
111 - Get Along Gang	15	5	6	7	8	9	10	
83 AL M-P	8	5	6	7	8	9	10	
112 - Ghostbusters	20	5	6	7	8	9	10	
86 DE M-P	10	5	6	7	8	9	10	
113 - Giant Eagle	30	5	6	7	8	9	10	
78 TA		5	6	7	8	9	10	
114 - Girls & Boys on Scooters (Dome)	20	5	6	7	8	9	10	
87 TA M-P	10	5	6	7	8	9	10	
115 - Go Bots	15	5	6	7	8	9	10	
84 TH M-P	8	5	6	7	8	9	10	
116 - Golden Girl	15	5	6	7	8	9	10	
84 TH M-P	8	5	6	7	8	9	10	
117 - Goonies	35	5	6	7	8	9	10	
85 AL M-P	15	5	6	7	8	9	10	
118 - Green (Dome)	20	5	6	7	8	9	10	
73 AL G-P	12	5	6	7	8	9	10	
119 - Gumby	60	5	6	7	8	9	10	
86 TH M-P	20	5	6	7	8	9	10	
120 - Happy Meal	25	5	6	7	8	9	10	
89 FP		5	6	7	8	9	10	

121 - Hardee's	25	5	6	7	8	9	10	
80　　　TA　　　M-P	10	5	6	7	8	9	10	
122 - Harley-Davidson	55	5	6	7	8	9	10	
78　　　TA		5	6	7	8	9	10	
123 - Hello Kitty (Dome)	45	5	6	7	8	9	10	
84　　　JA　　　M-P	20	5	6	7	8	9	10	
124 - Herself the Elf	15	5	6	7	8	9	10	
82　　　TH　　　M-P	8	5	6	7	8	9	10	
125 - Hot Wheels	55	5	6	7	8	9	10	
84　　　TH　　　M-P	20	5	6	7	8	9	10	
126 - Howdy Doody (Dome)	80	5	6	7	8	9	10	
77　　　TH　　　M-P	35	5	6	7	8	9	10	
127 - Hugga Bunch	10	5	6	7	8	9	10	
84　　　ALH　　　M-P	5	5	6	7	8	9	10	
128 - Hulk (Dome)	40	5	6	7	8	9	10	
80　　　AL　　　M-P	15	5	6	7	8	9	10	
129 - Hungry Horace Hippo	20	5	6	7	8	9	10	
87　　　UK　　　M-P	10	5	6	7	8	9	10	
130 - Insects (Dome)	20	5	6	7	8	9	10	
90　　　UNK		5	6	7	8	9	10	
131 - Inspector Gadget	25	5	6	7	8	9	10	
83　　　TH　　　M-P	12	5	6	7	8	9	10	
132 - It's not just the Bus - Grayhound	60	5	6	7	8	9	10	
80　　　AL　　　M-P	25	5	6	7	8	9	10	
133 - Jabber Jaw	55	5	6	7	8	9	10	
77　　　TH　　　M-P	20	5	6	7	8	9	10	
134 - Jetsons (3-D Blue)	75	5	6	7	8	9	10	
87　　　SE　　　M-P	30	5	6	7	8	9	10	
135 - Jetsons (3-D Purple)	75	5	6	7	8	9	10	
87　　　SE　　　M-P	30	5	6	7	8	9	10	

136 - Jetsons (Movie)	30	5	6	7	8	9	10	
90 AL M-P	15	5	6	7	8	9	10	
137 - Jetsons (Paper Picture)	110	5	6	7	8	9	10	
87 SE M-P	30	5	6	7	8	9	10	
138 - Jungle	20	5	6	7	8	9	10	
90 UNK		5	6	7	8	9	10	
139 - Kansas City Royals w/Coupon Book	40	5	6	7	8	9	10	
81 TA M-P	20	5	6	7	8	9	10	
140 - Karate	20	5	6	7	8	9	10	
80 TA M-P	8	5	6	7	8	9	10	
141 - Keebler	40	5	6	7	8	9	10	
78 TA M-P	20	5	6	7	8	9	10	
142 - Kellog's Corn Flakes	60	5	6	7	8	9	10	
78 TA M-P	30	5	6	7	8	9	10	
143 - Kellog's Rice Krispies Bars	55	5	6	7	8	9	10	
78 ALC G-P	20	5	6	7	8	9	10	
144 - Keny Cars	20	5	6	7	8	9	10	
86 ME M-P	12	5	6	7	8	9	10	
145 - Keny Children	20	5	6	7	8	9	10	
86 ME M-P	12	5	6	7	8	9	10	
146 - Kermit Frog Lunch	25	5	6	7	8	9	10	
88 TH M-P	8	5	6	7	8	9	10	
147 - Kermit's Scout Van	18	5	6	7	8	9	10	
89 SU		5	6	7	8	9	10	
148 - Kool-Aid Man	25	5	6	7	8	9	10	
86 TH M-P	10	5	6	7	8	9	10	
149 - L.A. Gear Club	25	5	6	7	8	9	10	
87 TA		5	6	7	8	9	10	
150 - Labyrinth	25	5	6	7	8	9	10	
86 TH M-P	12	5	6	7	8	9	10	

151 - Levi's	30	5	6	7	8	9	10	
85 TA M-P	15	5	6	7	8	9	10	
152 - Lisa Frank	15	5	6	7	8	9	10	
80 TH M-P	8	5	6	7	8	9	10	
153 - Little Orphan Annie	50	5	6	7	8	9	10	
73 TH M-P	20	5	6	7	8	9	10	
154 - Lolly's New Look (Merle Norman)	25	5	6	7	8	9	10	
85 TA		5	6	7	8	9	10	
155 - Looney Tunes Birthday Party (Blue)	20	5	6	7	8	9	10	
89 TH M-P	8	5	6	7	8	9	10	
156 - Looney Tunes Birthday Party (Red)	20	5	6	7	8	9	10	
89 TH M-P	8	5	6	7	8	9	10	
157 - Looney Tunes Dancing	25	5	6	7	8	9	10	
77 TH		5	6	7	8	9	10	
158 - Looney Tunes Playing Drum	25	5	6	7	8	9	10	
78 TH M-P	18	5	6	7	8	9	10	
159 - Looney Tunes Tasmanian Devil	25	5	6	7	8	9	10	
88 TH G-P	10	5	6	7	8	9	10	
160 - Los Angeles Olympics	25	5	6	7	8	9	10	
84 AL M-P	10	5	6	7	8	9	10	
161 - Lucy's Luncheonette	15	5	6	7	8	9	10	
81 TH M-P	8	5	6	7	8	9	10	
162 - Lunch Box (Enjoy Sports)	20	5	6	7	8	9	10	
85 TA G-P	8	5	6	7	8	9	10	
163 - Lunch Break	30	5	6	7	8	9	10	
86 TA M-P	15	5	6	7	8	9	10	
164 - Lunch Man w/Radio	35	5	6	7	8	9	10	
86 FD		5	6	7	8	9	10	
165 - Lunch Time w/Snoopy (Dome)	15	5	6	7	8	9	10	
81 TH M-P	8	5	6	7	8	9	10	

166 - Lunch'n Tunes Safari 86 FD	35	5 6 7 8 9 10 5 6 7 8 9 10	
167 - Lunch'n Tunes Singing Sandwich 86 FD	35	5 6 7 8 9 10 5 6 7 8 9 10	
168 - Lunchtime w/Clock (Front) 88 MK M-P	20 8	5 6 7 8 9 10 5 6 7 8 9 10	
169 - Lunchtime w/Clock (Top) 88 MK M-P	20 8	5 6 7 8 9 10 5 6 7 8 9 10	
170 - Mad Balls 86 AL M-P	25 10	5 6 7 8 9 10 5 6 7 8 9 10	
171 - Marimekko 80 TA G-P	20 8	5 6 7 8 9 10 5 6 7 8 9 10	
172 - Mariners 85 TA M-P	40 12	5 6 7 8 9 10 5 6 7 8 9 10	
173 - Marvel Super Heroes 90 TH M-P	20 10	5 6 7 8 9 10 5 6 7 8 9 10	
174 - Masters of the Universe 85 THC M-P	25 10	5 6 7 8 9 10 5 6 7 8 9 10	
175 - Max Headroom (Coke) 85 AL M-P	50 25	5 6 7 8 9 10 5 6 7 8 9 10	
176 - McDonalds TA	15	5 6 7 8 9 10 5 6 7 8 9 10	
177 - McDonalds TA	15	5 6 7 8 9 10 5 6 7 8 9 10	
178 - McDonalds (Give Away) TA	20	5 6 7 8 9 10 5 6 7 8 9 10	
179 - Menudo 84 TH M-P	20 10	5 6 7 8 9 10 5 6 7 8 9 10	
180 - Mermaid 89 TH G-P	15 8	5 6 7 8 9 10 5 6 7 8 9 10	

181 - Mickey & Donald	20	5	6	7	8	9	10	
84　AL　M-P	10	5	6	7	8	9	10	
182 - Mickey & Donald	25	5	6	7	8	9	10	
84　ALC　M-P	10	5	6	7	8	9	10	
183 - Mickey & Donald on See-Saw	12	5	6	7	8	9	10	
86　AL　M-P	5	5	6	7	8	9	10	
184 - Mickey & Minnie (Pink Car)	15	5	6	7	8	9	10	
88　AL　M-P	10	5	6	7	8	9	10	
185 - Mickey & the Bus	35	5	6	7	8	9	10	
	15	5	6	7	8	9	10	
186 - Mickey & the Gang	20	5	6	7	8	9	10	
89　TA　M-P	10	5	6	7	8	9	10	
187 - Mickey (Head)	30	5	6	7	8	9	10	
89　AL　M-P	5	5	6	7	8	9	10	
188 - Mickey (Mobile)	35	5	6	7	8	9	10	
78　TA		5	6	7	8	9	10	
189 - Mickey at City Zoo	12	5	6	7	8	9	10	
85　AL　M-P	5	5	6	7	8	9	10	
190 - Mickey on Swinging Bridge	15	5	6	7	8	9	10	
87　AL　M-P	8	5	6	7	8	9	10	
191 - Mickey Skate Boarding	18	5	6	7	8	9	10	
80　AL　M-P	8	5	6	7	8	9	10	
192 - Mighty Mouse	60	5	6	7	8	9	10	
79　TH　M-P	20	5	6	7	8	9	10	
193 - Minnesota Timber Wolves	45	5	6	7	8	9	10	
85　TA		5	6	7	8	9	10	
194 - Miss Piggy's Safari Van	20	5	6	7	8	9	10	
89　SU		5	6	7	8	9	10	
195 - Monster in My Pocket	30	5	6	7	8	9	10	
90　AL　M-P	10	5	6	7	8	9	10	

196 - Movie Monsters	80	5	6	7	8	9	10	
79 ALC M-P	45	5	6	7	8	9	10	
197 - Mr. T	25	5	6	7	8	9	10	
84 AL M-P	10	5	6	7	8	9	10	
198 - Munchie Tunes Bear w/Radio	45	5	6	7	8	9	10	
86 FD M-P	15	5	6	7	8	9	10	
199 - Munchie Tunes Punchie Pup w/Radio	45	5	6	7	8	9	10	
86 FD M-P	15	5	6	7	8	9	10	
200 - Munchie Tunes Robot w/Radio	45	5	6	7	8	9	10	
86 FD M-P	15	5	6	7	8	9	10	
201 - Muppets (Blue)	12	5	6	7	8	9	10	
82 TH M-P	5	5	6	7	8	9	10	
202 - Muppets (Dome)	20	5	6	7	8	9	10	
81 TH M-P	5	5	6	7	8	9	10	
203 - Muppets (Dome)	25	5	6	7	8	9	10	
80 THC G-P	15	5	6	7	8	9	10	
204 - Muppets (School Bus)	20	5	6	7	8	9	10	
89 UNK M-P		5	6	7	8	9	10	
205 - Nestle Quik	45	5	6	7	8	9	10	
80 TA M-P	20	5	6	7	8	9	10	
206 - New Kids on the Block (Pink or Orange)	10	5	6	7	8	9	10	
90 TH M-P	5	5	6	7	8	9	10	
207 - NHLPA	110	5	6	7	8	9	10	
74 ALC M-P	50	5	6	7	8	9	10	
208 - Noid	40	5	6	7	8	9	10	
81 TA		5	6	7	8	9	10	
209 - Nosy Bears	12	5	6	7	8	9	10	
88 AL M-P	8	5	6	7	8	9	10	
210 - Open for Lunch	30	5	6	7	8	9	10	
87 TA		5	6	7	8	9	10	

211 - Orange (Dome)	25	5	6	7	8	9	10	
81 **AL** **M-P**	12	5	6	7	8	9	10	
212 - Orange top-Yellow bottom (Dome)	25	5	6	7	8	9	10	
81 **AL** **M-P**	12	5	6	7	8	9	10	
213 - Paw Paws	20	5	6	7	8	9	10	
85 **HBT** **M-P**	10	5	6	7	8	9	10	
214 - Peanuts w/Snakes & Ladders Game	30	5	6	7	8	9	10	
80 **THE** **M-P**	12	5	6	7	8	9	10	
215 - Peanuts Weinie Roast	10	5	6	7	8	9	10	
85 **TH** **M-P**	5	5	6	7	8	9	10	
216 - Pee-Wee's Playhouse	25	5	6	7	8	9	10	
87 **TH** **G-P**	5	5	6	7	8	9	10	
217 - Peter Pan	85	5	6	7	8	9	10	
84 **TA** **M-P**	30	5	6	7	8	9	10	
218 - Pickle	175	5	6	7	8	9	10	
72 **FS**		5	6	7	8	9	10	
219 - Picnic with the Bears	25	5	6	7	8	9	10	
86 **TA** **M-P**	12	5	6	7	8	9	10	
220 - Pittsburgh Pirates	45	5	6	7	8	9	10	
88 **TA** **M-P**	15	5	6	7	8	9	10	
221 - Police Car	20	5	6	7	8	9	10	
85 **TA** **G-P**	10	5	6	7	8	9	10	
222 - Popeye	150	5	6	7	8	9	10	
64 **KST** **M-S**	60	5	6	7	8	9	10	
223 - Popeye & Son (3-D Red)	50	5	6	7	8	9	10	
87 **SE** **M-P**	20	5	6	7	8	9	10	
224 - Popeye & Son (3-D Yellow)	50	5	6	7	8	9	10	
87 **SE** **M-P**	20	5	6	7	8	9	10	
225 - Popeye & Son (Paper Picture)	65	5	6	7	8	9	10	
87 **SE** **M-P**	20	5	6	7	8	9	10	

226 - Popeye (Dome)	35	5 6 7 8 9 10	
79 AL M-P	15	5 6 7 8 9 10	
227 - Punky Brewster	20	5 6 7 8 9 10	
84 DE M-P	8	5 6 7 8 9 10	
228 - Pup Named Scooby-Doo	25	5 6 7 8 9 10	
88 AL M-P	15	5 6 7 8 9 10	
229 - Puppy	20	5 6 7 8 9 10	
87 TA		5 6 7 8 9 10	
230 - Q-Bert	25	5 6 7 8 9 10	
83 TH M-P	12	5 6 7 8 9 10	
231 - R.C. Races	25	5 6 7 8 9 10	
89 ALV M-P	10	5 6 7 8 9 10	
232 - Race Cars	20	5 6 7 8 9 10	
87 SE		5 6 7 8 9 10	
233 - Raggedy Ann & Andy	45	5 6 7 8 9 10	
88 AL M-P	20	5 6 7 8 9 10	
234 - Rainbow Brite	10	5 6 7 8 9 10	
83 TH M-P	5	5 6 7 8 9 10	
235 - Red (Dome)	25	5 6 7 8 9 10	
81 AL M-P	15	5 6 7 8 9 10	
236 - Red (Dome)	15	5 6 7 8 9 10	
80 IS		5 6 7 8 9 10	
237 - Red Barn (Dome)	25	5 6 7 8 9 10	
82 TH M-P	15	5 6 7 8 9 10	
238 - Robot Man	20	5 6 7 8 9 10	
84 TH M-P	10	5 6 7 8 9 10	
239 - Rocketeer	30	5 6 7 8 9 10	
90 AL M-P	10	5 6 7 8 9 10	
240 - Rocky	25	5 6 7 8 9 10	
77 TH M-P	10	5 6 7 8 9 10	

241 - Roller Games	25	5	6	7	8	9	10	
89　　TH　　M-P	10	5	6	7	8	9	10	
242 - S.W.A.T. (Dome)	45	5	6	7	8	9	10	
75　　TH　　M-P	15	5	6	7	8	9	10	
243 - School Bus	20	5	6	7	8	9	10	
86　　TA		5	6	7	8	9	10	
244 - School Bus Fancy Friends	20	5	6	7	8	9	10	
85　　TA　　G-P	10	5	6	7	8	9	10	
245 - Scooby-Doo	40	5	6	7	8	9	10	
73　　TH　　M-P	20	5	6	7	8	9	10	
246 - Scooby-Doo	35	5	6	7	8	9	10	
84　　AL　　M-P	20	5	6	7	8	9	10	
247 - Sesame Street	20	5	6	7	8	9	10	
85　　ALC　　M-P	10	5	6	7	8	9	10	
248 - Shirt Tales	10	5	6	7	8	9	10	
81　　TH　　M-P	5	5	6	7	8	9	10	
249 - Six Million Dollar Man(Back of Bobby Orr)	150	5	6	7	8	9	10	
74　　ALC　　M-P	50	5	6	7	8	9	10	
250 - Sky Commanders	15	5	6	7	8	9	10	
87　　TH　　G-P	5	5	6	7	8	9	10	
251 - Smurfette	10	5	6	7	8	9	10	
84　　TH　　M-P	8	5	6	7	8	9	10	
252 - Smurfs	15	5	6	7	8	9	10	
73　　THE　　M-P	8	5	6	7	8	9	10	
253 - Smurfs	10	5	6	7	8	9	10	
84　　TH　　M-P	8	5	6	7	8	9	10	
254 - Smurfs (Dome)	20	5	6	7	8	9	10	
81　　TH　　M-P	8	5	6	7	8	9	10	
255 - Smurfs Fishing	12	5	6	7	8	9	10	
84　　TH　　M-P	8	5	6	7	8	9	10	

		5	6	7	8	9	10	
256 - Snak Shot (Back of Blue)	35	5	6	7	8	9	10	
87 HU G-P	12	5	6	7	8	9	10	
257 - Snak Shot (Front of Green)	35	5	6	7	8	9	10	
87 HU G-P	12	5	6	7	8	9	10	
258 - Snoopy & Woodstock w/sports on back	25	5	6	7	8	9	10	
70 THE M-P	10	5	6	7	8	9	10	
259 - Snoopy & Woodstock w/sports on back	25	5	6	7	8	9	10	
80 THE M-P	10	5	6	7	8	9	10	
260 - Snoopy (Dome)	20	5	6	7	8	9	10	
78 TH M-P	10	5	6	7	8	9	10	
261 - Snorks	12	5	6	7	8	9	10	
84 TH M-P	5	5	6	7	8	9	10	
262 - Snow White	40	5	6	7	8	9	10	
80 AL M-P	15	5	6	7	8	9	10	
263 - Spaceman & Woman	40	5	6	7	8	9	10	
80 TA G-P	10	5	6	7	8	9	10	
264 - Spare Parts	35	5	6	7	8	9	10	
82 AL G-P	15	5	6	7	8	9	10	
265 - Sport Billy	30	5	6	7	8	9	10	
82 TH M-P	20	5	6	7	8	9	10	
266 - Sport Goofy	40	5	6	7	8	9	10	
86 AL M-P	15	5	6	7	8	9	10	
267 - Spot	20	5	6	7	8	9	10	
86 EN G-P	10	5	6	7	8	9	10	
268 - St. Louis Cardinals	40	5	6	7	8	9	10	
90 TA		5	6	7	8	9	10	
269 - Star Com U.S. Space Force	35	5	6	7	8	9	10	
87 TH M-P	15	5	6	7	8	9	10	
270 - Star Trek	35	5	6	7	8	9	10	
88 TH G-P	10	5	6	7	8	9	10	

271 - Star Trek	50	5	6	7	8	9	10	
89 TH M-P	20	5	6	7	8	9	10	
272 - Stop Overworked Student	25	5	6	7	8	9	10	
86 TA M-P	15	5	6	7	8	9	10	
273 - Strawberry Shortcake	10	5	6	7	8	9	10	
80 AL M-P	5	5	6	7	8	9	10	
274 - Styro Lunch Box	15	5	6	7	8	9	10	
80 UNK		5	6	7	8	9	10	
275 - Sunkist	30	5	6	7	8	9	10	
87 TA		5	6	7	8	9	10	
276 - Superhog (Lunch Box)	40	5	6	7	8	9	10	
89 TA M-P	25	5	6	7	8	9	10	
277 - Superhog (Sandwich Box)	20	5	6	7	8	9	10	
89 TA		5	6	7	8	9	10	
278 - Superman	25	5	6	7	8	9	10	
80 AL		5	6	7	8	9	10	
279 - Superman II (Dome)	40	5	6	7	8	9	10	
86 AL M-P	20	5	6	7	8	9	10	
280 - Talespin	15	5	6	7	8	9	10	
86 AL M-P	10	5	6	7	8	9	10	
281 - Tang Trio (Red)	35	5	6	7	8	9	10	
88 TH G-P	8	5	6	7	8	9	10	
282 - Tang Trio (Yellow)	35	5	6	7	8	9	10	
88 TH G-P	8	5	6	7	8	9	10	
283 - Taxi	20	5	6	7	8	9	10	
85 TA G-P	5	5	6	7	8	9	10	
284 - Thundarr the Barbarian (Dome)	25	5	6	7	8	9	10	
81 AL M-P	10	5	6	7	8	9	10	
285 - Timeless Tales	10	5	6	7	8	9	10	
89 AL M-P	5	5	6	7	8	9	10	

286 - Tiny Toon 90　　TH　　M-P	10 5	5　6　7　8　9　10 5　6　7　8　9　10						
287 - To Market We Go 85　　TA　　M-P	25 15	5　6　7　8　9　10 5　6　7　8　9　10						
288 - Tom & Jerry 89　　AL　　M-P	30 15	5　6　7　8　9　10 5　6　7　8　9　10						
289 - Tommy Teaddy (Blue) 87　　TA　　G-P	20 8	5　6　7　8　9　10 5　6　7　8　9　10						
290 - Tommy Teaddy (Pink) 87　　TA　　G-P	20 8	5　6　7　8　9　10 5　6　7　8　9　10						
291 - Toronto Blue Jays 88　　TA　　M-P	35 15	5　6　7　8　9　10 5　6　7　8　9　10						
292 - Train 88　　TA	15	5　6　7　8　9　10 5　6　7　8　9　10						
293 - Transformers 86　　AL　　M-P	15 6	5　6　7　8　9　10 5　6　7　8　9　10						
294 - Transformers (Dome) 85　　ALC　　G-P	35 10	5　6　7　8　9　10 5　6　7　8　9　10						
295 - Tropicana 89　　TA　　M-P	40 15	5　6　7　8　9　10 5　6　7　8　9　10						
296 - Tubular 80　　TA　　M-P	50 20	5　6　7　8　9　10 5　6　7　8　9　10						
297 - Turquoise 　　AL　　G-P	20 10	5　6　7　8　9　10 5　6　7　8　9　10						
298 - Turtles 90　　TH　　G-P	10 5	5　6　7　8　9　10 5　6　7　8　9　10						
299 - Tweety & Sylvester 86　　TH　　M-P	45 20	5　6　7　8　9　10 5　6　7　8　9　10						
300 - Up, Up & Away 86　　TA　　M-P	30 15	5　6　7　8　9　10 5　6　7　8　9　10						

301 - Warning High Voltage Genius	30	5	6	7	8	9	10	
86 TA M-P	25	5	6	7	8	9	10	
302 - Wayne Gretzky (Blue)	95	5	6	7	8	9	10	
80 AL M-P	30	5	6	7	8	9	10	
303 - Wayne Gretzky (Dome)	110	5	6	7	8	9	10	
80 AL M-P	30	5	6	7	8	9	10	
304 - Wayne Gretzky (Orange)	95	5	6	7	8	9	10	
80 AL M-P	30	5	6	7	8	9	10	
305 - Where's Waldo	10	5	6	7	8	9	10	
90 TH M-P	5	5	6	7	8	9	10	
306 - White (Dome)	30	5	6	7	8	9	10	
TA		5	6	7	8	9	10	
307 - Who Framed Roger Rabbit (Red)	20	5	6	7	8	9	10	
87 TH M-P	10	5	6	7	8	9	10	
308 - Who Framed Roger Rabbit (Yellow)	20	5	6	7	8	9	10	
87 TH M-P	10	5	6	7	8	9	10	
309 - Wild Fire	15	5	6	7	8	9	10	
86 AL M-P	8	5	6	7	8	9	10	
310 - Wizard of OZ	60	5	6	7	8	9	10	
89 AL M-P	25	5	6	7	8	9	10	
311 - Wonder Woman Jr.	65	5	6	7	8	9	10	
81 ME		5	6	7	8	9	10	
312 - Woody Woodpecker	45	5	6	7	8	9	10	
84 UNK M-P	20	5	6	7	8	9	10	
313 - Wrinkles	12	5	6	7	8	9	10	
84 TH M-P	7	5	6	7	8	9	10	
314 - Wuzzles	15	5	6	7	8	9	10	
85 AL M-P	10	5	6	7	8	9	10	
315 - WWF	20	5	6	7	8	9	10	
86 TH M-P	10	5	6	7	8	9	10	

316 - Yellow & Orange (Dome)	**25**	5	6	7	8	9	10	
81 **UNK** **M-P**	**15**	5	6	7	8	9	10	
317 - Yellow (Dome)	**25**	5	6	7	8	9	10	
81 **AL**		5	6	7	8	9	10	
318 - Yellow Jafra w/give-away samples	**30**	5	6	7	8	9	10	
89 **AL**		5	6	7	8	9	10	
319 - Yogi's Treasure Hunt (3-D Green)	**55**	5	6	7	8	9	10	
87 **SE** **M-P**	**30**	5	6	7	8	9	10	
320 - Yogi's Treasure Hunt (3-D Pink)	**55**	5	6	7	8	9	10	
87 **SE** **M-P**	**30**	5	6	7	8	9	10	
321 - Yogi's Treasure Hunt (Paper Picture)	**75**	5	6	7	8	9	10	
87 **SE** **M-P**	**30**	5	6	7	8	9	10	
322 - Zazoo	**25**	5	6	7	8	9	10	
UNK **M-P**	**10**	5	6	7	8	9	10	

1 - Backgammon 60's **KST** HOLTEMP	160 40	5 6 7 8 9 10 5 6 7 8 9 10						
2 - Band Aid 80's **UNK**	150 20	5 6 7 8 9 10 5 6 7 8 9 10						
3 - Barbarino 77 **AL** **M-P**	250 30	5 6 7 8 9 10 5 6 7 8 9 10						
4 - Beatles 66 **AL** **M-S/G**	625 250	5 6 7 8 9 10 5 6 7 8 9 10						
5 - Blue Denim 70 **KST** **M**	45 30	5 6 7 8 9 10 5 6 7 8 9 10						
6 - Blue Gingham 75 **AL** **M-P**	45 30	5 6 7 8 9 10 5 6 7 8 9 10						
7 - Blue Jeans 74 **KST**	55 30	5 6 7 8 9 10 5 6 7 8 9 10						
8 - Brown 72 **KST**	60 25	5 6 7 8 9 10 5 6 7 8 9 10						
9 - Brown (Box) 72 **AL**	55 20	5 6 7 8 9 10 5 6 7 8 9 10						
10 - Calico 80 **AL** **M-P**	70 30	5 6 7 8 9 10 5 6 7 8 9 10						
11 - Can of Flowers 70's **AL** **M-P**	50 35	5 6 7 8 9 10 5 6 7 8 9 10						
12 - Can of Flowers w/Golf Ball 70's **AL** **M-P**	80 50	5 6 7 8 9 10 5 6 7 8 9 10						
13 - Candy's 73 **KST**	150	5 6 7 8 9 10 5 6 7 8 9 10						
14 - Charlie's Angels 78 **AL** **M-P**	160 30	5 6 7 8 9 10 5 6 7 8 9 10						
15 - Coca-Cola (Box) 88 **UNK**	55	5 6 7 8 9 10 5 6 7 8 9 10						

16 - College Pennant	170	5	6	7	8	9	10	
70's UNK	35	5	6	7	8	9	10	
17 - Dark Brown	65	5	6	7	8	9	10	
70's UNK SYO	20	5	6	7	8	9	10	
18 - Dark Brown(Leather)	65	5	6	7	8	9	10	
60's KST M-S/G	30	5	6	7	8	9	10	
19 - Diagonal	85	5	6	7	8	9	10	
74 AL		5	6	7	8	9	10	
20 - Doggie Bag	160	5	6	7	8	9	10	
78 KST		5	6	7	8	9	10	
21 - Donny & Marie (Long Hair)	125	5	6	7	8	9	10	
77 AL M-P	30	5	6	7	8	9	10	
22 - Donny & Marie (Short Hair)	125	5	6	7	8	9	10	
78 AL M-P	30	5	6	7	8	9	10	
23 - Funny Fish	185	5	6	7	8	9	10	
75 AL M	45	5	6	7	8	9	10	
24 - Gadabout	110	5	6	7	8	9	10	
69 AL M-P	45	5	6	7	8	9	10	
25 - Gadabout	110	5	6	7	8	9	10	
71 AL M-P	45	5	6	7	8	9	10	
26 - Go Go	245	5	6	7	8	9	10	
66 AL M-S/G	60	5	6	7	8	9	10	
27 - Green w/Gold Bands	60	5	6	7	8	9	10	
68 AL		5	6	7	8	9	10	
28 - Holly Hobbie	85	5	6	7	8	9	10	
73 AL M-P	10	5	6	7	8	9	10	
29 - Holly Hobbie	95	5	6	7	8	9	10	
78 AL M-P	20	5	6	7	8	9	10	
30 - Jonathan Livingston Seagull	175	5	6	7	8	9	10	
74 AL M-P	25	5	6	7	8	9	10	

31 - Krazy Daisy's (Brown)	65	5	6	7	8	9	10	
70　KST　M	35	5	6	7	8	9	10	
32 - Krazy Daisy's (Green)	65	5	6	7	8	9	10	
71　KST　M-S/G	30	5	6	7	8	9	10	
33 - Laurita Lunchita	110	5	6	7	8	9	10	
50's　AL　M	40	5	6	7	8	9	10	
34 - Laurita Lunchita	110	5	6	7	8	9	10	
50's　AL　M	40	5	6	7	8	9	10	
35 - Leather Di	55	5	6	7	8	9	10	
65　AL　S/G	30	5	6	7	8	9	10	
36 - Life Savers	110	5	6	7	8	9	10	
70's　UNK		5	6	7	8	9	10	
37 - Light Brown (Leather)	65	5	6	7	8	9	10	
60's　KST　M	30	5	6	7	8	9	10	
38 - Love	140	5	6	7	8	9	10	
70's　UNK		5	6	7	8	9	10	
39 - Love (1 Girl)	125	5	6	7	8	9	10	
75　AL　M-P	45	5	6	7	8	9	10	
40 - Love (3 Kids)	135	5	6	7	8	9	10	
74　AL　M-P	45	5	6	7	8	9	10	
41 - Love (5 Kids)	160	5	6	7	8	9	10	
72　AL　M-P	45	5	6	7	8	9	10	
42 - Mardi Gras	60	5	6	7	8	9	10	
71　AL　M-P	25	5	6	7	8	9	10	
43 - Mary Poppins	160	5	6	7	8	9	10	
66　AL　M-S/G	50	5	6	7	8	9	10	
44 - Medallion	140	5	6	7	8	9	10	
65　AL　M-S/G	55	5	6	7	8	9	10	
45 - Mod Miss (Black)	120	5	6	7	8	9	10	
71　AL　M	45	5	6	7	8	9	10	

46 - Mod Miss (Blue)	120	5	6	7	8	9	10	
70 AL M	45	5	6	7	8	9	10	
47 - Mushrooms	130	5	6	7	8	9	10	
73 AL M-P	35	5	6	7	8	9	10	
48 - Mushrooms (Pink)	155	5	6	7	8	9	10	
73 AL M-P/S	35	5	6	7	8	9	10	
49 - Orange Swirl	220	5	6	7	8	9	10	
65 AL	95	5	6	7	8	9	10	
50 - Owls	55	5	6	7	8	9	10	
70's AL M-P	40	5	6	7	8	9	10	
51 - Patches	50	5	6	7	8	9	10	
72 KST S/G	30	5	6	7	8	9	10	
52 - Patches (Tall)	50	5	6	7	8	9	10	
73 KST P	20	5	6	7	8	9	10	
53 - Picadilly Green	80	5	6	7	8	9	10	
70 AL M-P	25	5	6	7	8	9	10	
54 - Picadilly Green	80	5	6	7	8	9	10	
71 AL M-P	25	5	6	7	8	9	10	
55 - Princess	140	5	6	7	8	9	10	
62 AL M	60	5	6	7	8	9	10	
56 - Pussycats	220	5	6	7	8	9	10	
68 AL M-P	70	5	6	7	8	9	10	
57 - Pyschedelic	165	5	6	7	8	9	10	
70 AL P	45	5	6	7	8	9	10	
58 - Pyschedelic (Blue)	80	5	6	7	8	9	10	
68 KST M-S/G	35	5	6	7	8	9	10	
59 - Pyschedelic (Blue)	80	5	6	7	8	9	10	
70 KST M-S/G	35	5	6	7	8	9	10	
60 - Raggedy Ann & Andy	110	5	6	7	8	9	10	
73 AL M-S/G	25	5	6	7	8	9	10	

61 - Red Flower	45	5	6	7	8	9	10	
70's AL M-P	35	5	6	7	8	9	10	
62 - Red Flower w/tennis racquet	80	5	6	7	8	9	10	
70's AL M-P	50	5	6	7	8	9	10	
63 - Red Plaid (Diagonal Pattern)	110	5	6	7	8	9	10	
70's UNK		5	6	7	8	9	10	
64 - Red Roses	90	5	6	7	8	9	10	
68 KST M-S/G	45	5	6	7	8	9	10	
65 - Red Roses	90	5	6	7	8	9	10	
70 KST M-S/G	45	5	6	7	8	9	10	
66 - Rose Needlepoint	120	5	6	7	8	9	10	
72 AL M-P	40	5	6	7	8	9	10	
67 - Sixteen Dots	45	5	6	7	8	9	10	
68 AL S/G	15	5	6	7	8	9	10	
68 - Snoopy	85	5	6	7	8	9	10	
77 KST M-P	20	5	6	7	8	9	10	
69 - Sophisticate	110	5	6	7	8	9	10	
70 AL M-P	45	5	6	7	8	9	10	
70 - Speedy Turtle	180	5	6	7	8	9	10	
78 KST		5	6	7	8	9	10	
71 - Stallions	180	5	6	7	8	9	10	
62 AL S/G	15	5	6	7	8	9	10	
72 - Stars & Stripes	175	5	6	7	8	9	10	
70 KST M-S/G	60	5	6	7	8	9	10	
73 - Strawberries	45	5	6	7	8	9	10	
70's AL M-P	35	5	6	7	8	9	10	
74 - Sweeter Days	140	5	6	7	8	9	10	
73 KST M	40	5	6	7	8	9	10	
75 - Tartan	60	5	6	7	8	9	10	
62 AL M-S/G	30	5	6	7	8	9	10	

76 - Tartan 70 AL M-P	45 30	5 6 7 8 9 10 5 6 7 8 9 10	
77 - Tennis Motif 76 AL M-P	180 40	5 6 7 8 9 10 5 6 7 8 9 10	
78 - The Sophisticate 69 AL M-P	110 45	5 6 7 8 9 10 5 6 7 8 9 10	
79 - Town & Country 65 AL M-S/G	65 40	5 6 7 8 9 10 5 6 7 8 9 10	
80 - Town & Country 68 AL M-P	65 40	5 6 7 8 9 10 5 6 7 8 9 10	
81 - Twiggy 67 AL M-S/G	260 65	5 6 7 8 9 10 5 6 7 8 9 10	
82 - U.S. Mail 75 AL	180 30	5 6 7 8 9 10 5 6 7 8 9 10	
83 - White Dots 69 AL M-P	55 45	5 6 7 8 9 10 5 6 7 8 9 10	
84 - Wise Guy 77 KST	145	5 6 7 8 9 10 5 6 7 8 9 10	
85 - World Travler 61 AL	160	5 6 7 8 9 10 5 6 7 8 9 10	

1 - Annie Oakley		370	5	6	7	8	9	10	
50's AL M-S/G		175	5	6	7	8	9	10	
2 - Blue Square		75	5	6	7	8	9	10	
50's AL M-S/G		30	5	6	7	8	9	10	
3 - Girl Scout		140	5	6	7	8	9	10	
50's AL M-S/G		60	5	6	7	8	9	10	
4 - Girl Scout (Box)		150	5	6	7	8	9	10	
60 AL M-S/G		50	5	6	7	8	9	10	
5 - Lunch-in-ette (Plaid)		30	5	6	7	8	9	10	
50's PP			5	6	7	8	9	10	
6 - Navy & Red		90	5	6	7	8	9	10	
50's AL M-S/G		40	5	6	7	8	9	10	
7 - Pink & Teal		80	5	6	7	8	9	10	
50's AL M-S/G		35	5	6	7	8	9	10	
8 - Plaid		55	5	6	7	8	9	10	
50's AL M-S/G		25	5	6	7	8	9	10	
9 - Red Bottom		70	5	6	7	8	9	10	
50's AL M-S/G		30	5	6	7	8	9	10	

1 - Maroon Raccoon 84 AL P	20	5 6 7 8 9 10 5 6 7 8 9 10	
2 - Mickey Mouse 73 AL P	60	5 6 7 8 9 10 5 6 7 8 9 10	
3 - Pirates 84 AL P	25	5 6 7 8 9 10 5 6 7 8 9 10	
4 - Round Up 84 AL P	30	5 6 7 8 9 10 5 6 7 8 9 10	
5 - Tony Tiger (Be Safety Smart) 85 TA P	20	5 6 7 8 9 10 5 6 7 8 9 10	
6 - Tootsie Roll 78 AL P	25	5 6 7 8 9 10 5 6 7 8 9 10	

1 - Pre School	10	5	6	7	8	9	10	
FP M-P	4	5	6	7	8	9	10	
2 - Red (Dome)	5	5	6	7	8	9	10	
FP Blue	2	5	6	7	8	9	10	
3 - Red Barn Playset	8	5	6	7	8	9	10	
FP M-P	4	5	6	7	8	9	10	
4 - Red Top (Dome)	5	5	6	7	8	9	10	
FP M-P	2	5	6	7	8	9	10	
5 - Salt & Pepper Set (Ceramic)	10	5	6	7	8	9	10	
UNK		5	6	7	8	9	10	
6 - Yellow Top (Dome)	5	5	6	7	8	9	10	
FP M-P	2	5	6	7	8	9	10	

Ceramics

1 - Ceramic Dome Cookie Jar UNK	35	5 6 7 8 9 10 5 6 7 8 9 10	
2 - Ceramic Lunch Box Cookie Jar UNK	30	5 6 7 8 9 10 5 6 7 8 9 10	